Finding dialogue in boo

Recognise dialogue and write speech.

Find a page in your favourite reading book that has characters speaking to each other.

Draw a picture of each character and write what they say in speech bubbles.

A bird riddle

Read information to find out the answers.

Fact file: blackbirds and song thrushes

FOOD – Blackbirds eat insects and worms in summer and berries in winter. Song thrushes eat snails by banging their shells against a stone.

HABITAT (where they live) – Blackbirds nest in hedges and in small trees. Song thrushes nest in hedges, bushes or trees, or among ivy on buildings or banks.

EGGS – Blackbirds' eggs are blue–green with brown specks and there are usually three to five of them. Song thrushes usually lay four to five eggs that are blue spotted with black.

SONG – The male blackbird perches on a tree to sing his loud, clear song. The male song thrush sings his loud, short song over and over again from high up in a tree.

A hedgerow bird riddle

An ivy nester
A snail breaker
A short tune singer
With black spotted eggs
Who am I?

Read the fact file and the riddle. Which bird is the riddle about? Write your own riddle about a blackbird below.

A _____ nester

A _____ eater

A _____ singer

With _____ eggs

Who am I?

Answer – a song thrush

Homework Book 3

Hazel Willard

3

My map

Create a map.

Make a map of a place you know really well. Think about the road that leads up to it and the places you would see around it.

Label your map with interesting descriptive words and phrases.

Welcome to your new home!

Write a card to a story character.

Design a card welcoming Charlie to his new home. Draw a picture of his new home. Fill in the bubbles with the good things about his new home.

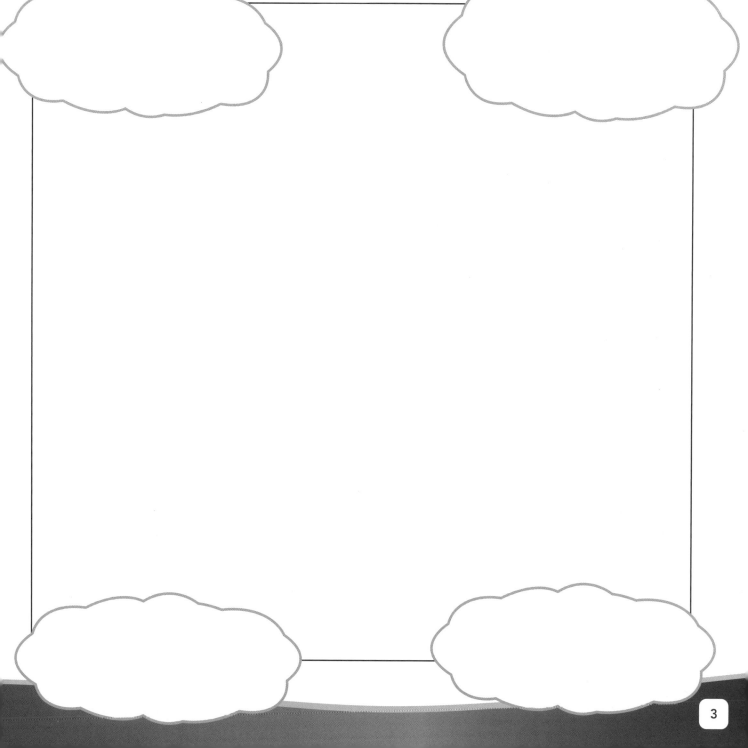

Ivy cottage

> **Write a description of Ivy Cottage.**

Write a description of Ivy Cottage. Include a description of where it is, what the outside looks like and what you think it's like inside.

Speech verbs word search

Identify speech verbs.

Find ten speech verbs in this square. Circle the verbs you find. Words go from left to right. The first one is done for you.

s	a	s	a	i	d	n	c	y	e	r
a	s	k	e	d	u	v	k	e	m	u
g	c	v	y	e	l	l	e	d	d	t
e	a	n	n	o	u	n	c	e	d	r
e	x	p	l	a	i	n	e	d	i	m
t	e	z	n	s	h	o	u	t	e	d
w	h	i	s	p	e	r	e	d	u	r
s	c	r	i	e	d	f	e	m	x	i
t	y	u	r	e	p	l	i	e	d	j
a	a	n	s	w	e	r	e	d	n	s

Design your own word search square on a sheet of paper, using movement verbs like *jump*. Use at least ten verbs in your square.

Verbs for speaking

Use verbs and punctuation for speech.

Use these verbs to complete the sentences.

said	cried	shouted

1 "I've hurt my leg," _____ the little girl.

2 "Hip, hip, hooray!"_____ the children.

3 "It's very hot today," _____ the boy to his mum.

Add speech marks and use these verbs to complete the sentences.

asked	answered	explained

1 Did you see it yourself? _____ the police officer.

2 No, my brother Tim did, _____ Laura.

3 I saw it when I was riding my bike, _____ Tim.

Choose five speech verbs and write five sentences of your own using the correct punctuation for writing speech. Use a separate sheet of paper.

Design a book cover

Design a cover for a non-fiction book.

Use the fact file on page 8 to help you design a cover for a non-fiction book about a blackbird or a song thrush.

An animal spidergram

Make notes about an animal on a spidergram.

Fill in this spidergram for an animal of your choice. Think about what you want to find out and write notes for each heading. Add more headings if you need to.

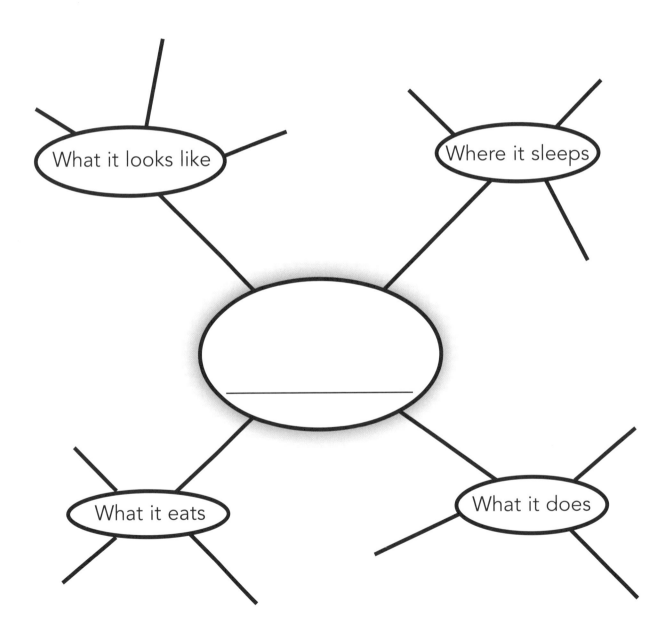

What it looks like

Where it sleeps

What it eats

What it does

Write a tongue twister

> **Use alliteration to write a tongue twister.**

Alliteration means using two or more words together that begin with the same letter or sound. For example: *She sells sea shells on the sea shore.*

A sentence like this is called a **tongue twister**.

1 Write the rest of this tongue twister using only the words *fish*, *fresh* and *fried*.

You can have

Fresh fish fried

Or _____ fresh fish

Or fish fresh _____

Or _____

2 Write a tongue twister using these words:

snow slipping slowly sideways

Put them in any order to make four lines of a tongue twister.

_____

_____

_____

_____

My night time nasty

Label a drawing with adjectives.

Draw a picture of what a night time nasty might look like. Label your drawing with adjectives and other words to describe your picture.

A certificate for bravery

Think about words that describe acts of bravery.

In the story of Odysseus and Polyphemus, Odysseus saved some of his crew from being killed by the Cyclops. His crew were so grateful that they gave him a certificate for bravery.

trick

blinding

sheep

cave

safely

hiding

Fill in the certificate. Write one brave thing that Odysseus did to save his crew. Use the words in the box to help you.

 Fill in the certificate. Write two brave things that Odysseus did to save his crew. Use the words in the box to help you.

THIS CERTIFICATE GOES TO ODYSSEUS FOR

_____

_____

_____

_____

_____

_____.

SIGNED_____

The Sparrow and the Ostrich

Use a story hand to tell a fable.

❶ Make a plan of the fable *The Sparrow and the Ostrich*.

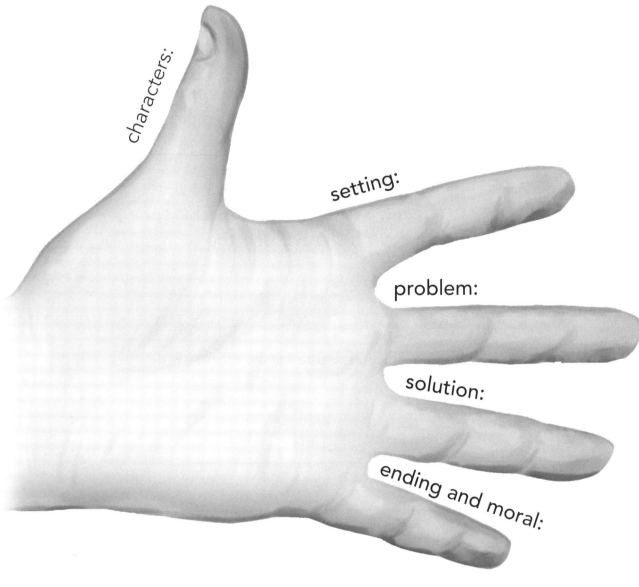

characters:

setting:

problem:

solution:

ending and moral:

❷ Decide which fingers the following information should go on and add it:

- Ostrich boasting to Sparrow
- a hot country
- pride comes before a fall

- Ostrich and Sparrow
- hunters kill Ostrich

❸ Use your story hand to help you tell the fable to someone.

The Birth of the Sun

Tell a creation story.

❶ Fill in the writing frame about the creation myth *The Birth of the Sun*.

Characters	brolga
	emu
	kookaburra
Setting	
Problem	
Solution	
Ending	

❷ Use your writing frame to tell the story to a friend or someone in your family.

Finding your home

Give written directions.

Give your friend directions from school to your home.
Write down the directions in the correct order.

Useful words

turn, left, right, next, straight on, over the bridge, down the hill, round the corner, after the shops, through the tunnel, before the, traffic lights.

Using imperative verbs

Identify imperative or "bossy" verbs.

Read the method section of the recipe for chocolate coconut balls.

Method

1   Mix coconut and sugar with the milk. If coconut is very dry, use less than the quantity given, or sweets may go hard.

2   Make small balls from the mixture.

3   Melt chocolate in a small basin over a pan of simmering water.

4   To coat the balls, drop them into the melted chocolate, lift each one out with a fork and tap it on the edge of the bowl to allow excess chocolate to drop off.

5   Put balls on waxed paper to set.

from **Divali** *by* **Howard Marsh**

---

❶ Underline all the imperative verbs – the verbs which tell you what you **must** do.

❷ Make a list of all the verbs you found.

_____   _____

_____   _____

_____   _____

❸ Choose a recipe of your own. How many imperative verbs can you find? List them on a sheet of paper.

Instructions for a robot

Write instructions clearly and in sequence.

Imagine you own a robot that can do your jobs for you.

Write a set of instructions telling a robot how to make your bed. Include a title and a purpose and remember to number your instructions. Don't forget to use imperative verbs.

Tip: Try saying the instructions aloud to yourself first.

Words with sounds

Use onomatopoeia in your writing.

Onomatopoeic words sound like the thing they represent, like *bang*, *crash*, *moo* and *quack*.

Design an advertisement for a breakfast cereal. Use three onomatopoeic words so that people will remember it. You can use words from the box or use your own.

crackle	slurp	fizz	pop

Find out about Roald Dahl

> **Research information about Roald Dahl.**

Find out about the life of Roald Dahl, for example by looking at the covers of his books, websites, covers of DVDs and audio books. Fill in the information below.

Date and place of birth:

Date of death:

Early life:

Later life:

Books by Roald Dahl:

Waiting in the dark

Describe how a fictional character feels.

Imagine how Danny feels sitting in the car waiting for the police to arrive. Draw a picture of him and label it with words describing his feelings. Use the words in the box, or use your own.

frightened   worried   shivery   scared   excited   nervous

A letter from Mr Twit

Write a letter.

Imagine you are Mr Twit. Use the planning frame to write a letter to an agony aunt asking her how to stop Mrs Twit playing tricks on you. (An agony aunt is a writer in a newspaper or magazine who gives advice to people with a problem.) Plan what you will say, then write your letter on a separate sheet of paper.

Address and date
Greeting (Dear Aunty_____,)
Paragraph 1 (information about you and Mrs Twit)
Paragraph 2 (the problem)
Closing sentence (ask for advice)
End greeting (Yours sincerely,)

Girl finds bottle in loft

Retell what happened to Jacqueline Hyde.

Imagine you have heard a news report on the television about how Jacqueline Hyde found a strange bottle of liquid in her grandma's attic and what happened to her.

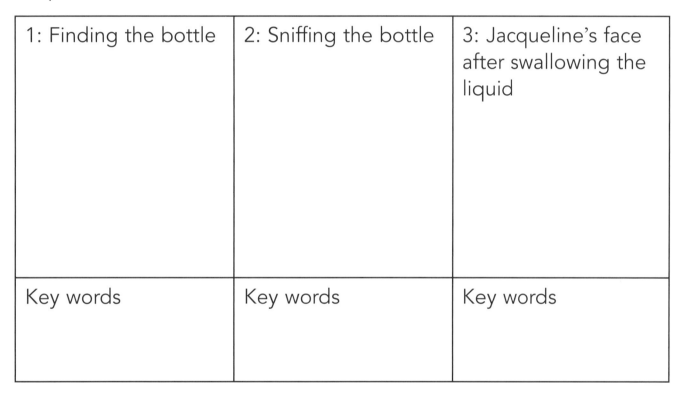

❶ Draw three pictures and write key words about the picture underneath.

1: Finding the bottle	2: Sniffing the bottle	3: Jacqueline's face after swallowing the liquid
Key words	Key words	Key words

❷ Write an email to a friend telling them what happened to Jacqueline when she drank the liquid.

Making a character portrait

> **Record information about a character on a portrait.**

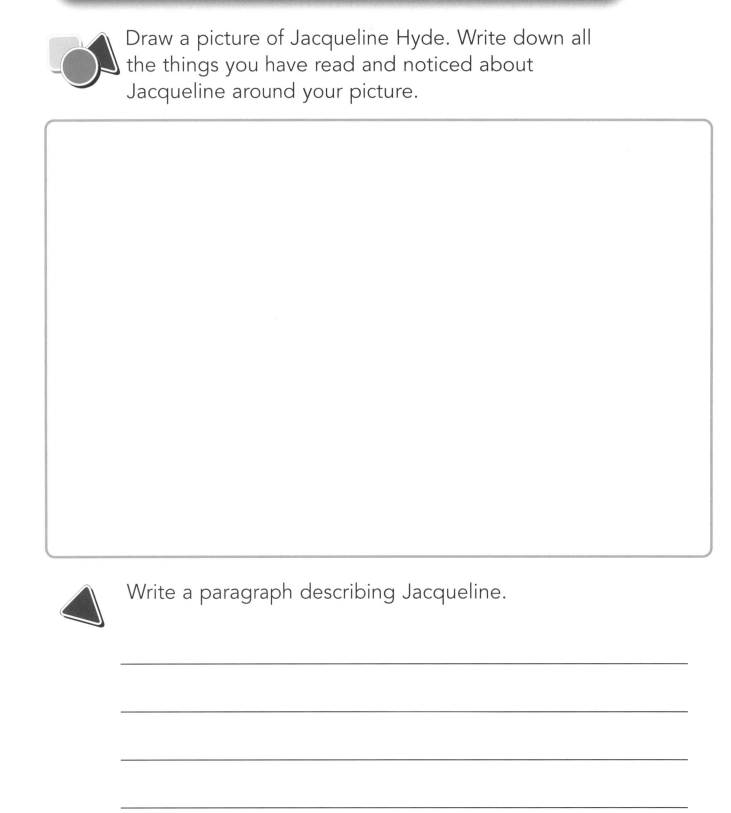 Draw a picture of Jacqueline Hyde. Write down all the things you have read and noticed about Jacqueline around your picture.

Write a paragraph describing Jacqueline.

_____

_____

_____

_____

Skull Island book cover

Create a book cover.

 Create your own cover for *Skull Island*. Remember to include the title, author's name (Lesley Sims) and illustrator's name (your name).

 Write a blurb for *Skull Island* on a separate sheet of paper. A blurb is a paragraph about the book that gives some information about the story.

Festival interview

Find out information about a festival.

Ask a friend or member of your family about a festival they enjoy celebrating. Fill in the chart below and add a question of your own in the space at the bottom.

Question	Answer
What is the name of the festival?	
When does it take place?	
Why does it take place?	
How long does it last?	
What special things happen?	
What do you enjoy most about the festival?	

Jumbled words

Use alphabetical order to sort words.

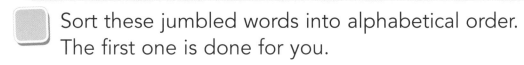

☐ Sort these jumbled words into alphabetical order. The first one is done for you.

cat   mouse   dog   bird   kitten   puppy   gerbil   rabbit

1 bird _____   5 _____

2 _____   6 _____

3 _____   7 _____

4 _____   8 _____

⬤ Sort these jumbled words into alphabetical order.

tiger   cheetah   cat   lion   leopard   lynx   elephant   emu

1 _____   5 _____

2 _____   6 _____

3 _____   7 _____

4 _____   8 _____

▲ Sort these words into alphabetical order.

dove   beetle   dolphin   camel   bear   dog   bison   beaver

1 _____   5 _____

2 _____   6 _____

3 _____   7 _____

4 _____   8 _____

Design a poster

Use persuasive imperative verbs.

Design a poster for a special festival or fête.

Think about all the things people would see, hear, smell and do. You can use the words in the box, or use your own.

Useful words

come   see   hear

smell   join in

In my home

Practise alphabetical order.

Write down a list of your favourite toys and games in the left-hand column. Sort them into alphabetical order and write them out again in the right-hand column. If any of the toys begin with the same letter, look at the second letter.

Favourite toys	Alphabetical order
❶	❶
❷	❷
❸	❸
❹	❹
❺	❺
❻	❻

Performing poems aloud

> **Think about and practise performing poems aloud.**

Practise reciting this poem. When you're ready, perform it to a friend or member of your family.

Night Time Nasties

Sometimes at night
When sleep won't come,
I hear strange noises that make my flesh numb.

The tick, tock, tick of the clock in the hall
Is the rhythm of feet as they stealthily fall,
Creeping, closer towards my bed.

But I know it's only in my head.

Long shadows of leaves on the window pane
Is a demon creature climbing the drain,
Clawing, closer towards my bed.

But I know it's only in my head.

The swish of the tyres on the busy M3
Is the cloak of a shadow man swirling round me,
Creeping closer towards my bed.

But I know it's only in my head.

The whistles and grunts of dad as he snores
Is a raging beast with raucous roars,
Charging closer towards my bed.

But I know it's only in my head.

I know it's only in my head
But the nasties are nudging towards my bed.
They thrive in the dark, the velvety black.

But they'll disappear at daylight's crack
When the first blackbird chatters.
They'll shiver and sigh,
Fading away, as they wither and die.

But they're waiting to pounce,
They're ready to bite.

Quickly, quickly, turn on the light!

Riddles

Write some funny riddles using homonyms.

Homonyms are words that sound the same but have different meanings.

Here is a riddle made from the homonym *peak*.

> What's the *busiest time at the top of a mountain?*
>
> Answer: Peak time!

What are the two meanings of this homonym?

1 _____

2 _____

Choose the right homonym to answer these riddles.

week/weak

What part of the month has the least energy?

Answer: The _____

tail/tale

Why is the cat's tail the most interesting part of its body?

Answer: Because it has a _____

sea/see

Why did the sea crash into the rocks?

Answer: Because it couldn't _____ them.

stair/stare

What did the staircase say to the step?

Answer: It's rude to _____.

Published by Collins
An imprint of HarperCollins*Publishers*
77–85 Fulham Palace Road
Hammersmith
London
W6 8JB

© HarperCollins*Publishers* Limited 2008

Author: Hazel Willard
Series editor: Kay Hiatt

10 9 8

ISBN 978 0 00 722716 7

British Library Cataloguing in Publication Data
A Catalogue record for this publication is available from the British Library.

Illustrations: Becky Blake, Shirley Chiang, Tim Archbold, Kev Hopgood, Sarah Horne

Photographs: p20, top left: Camera Press

Every effort has been made to trace copyright holders and to obtain their permission for the use of copyright material. The authors and publishers will gladly receive any information enabling them to rectify any error or omission in subsequent editions.

Browse the complete Collins catalogue at
www.collinseducation.com

Printed in China

ISBN 978-0-00-722716-7

9 780007 227167